Most Popular Classical Melodies
FOR EASY CLASSICAL GUITAR

Arranged by Mark Phillips

Contents

To access audio visit:
www.halleonard.com/mylibrary

5181-5533-4010-6231

ISBN 978-1-60378-148-0

Visit Hal Leonard Online at
www.halleonard.com

Andante Cantabile

Peter Il'yich Tchaikovsky

Moderately slow

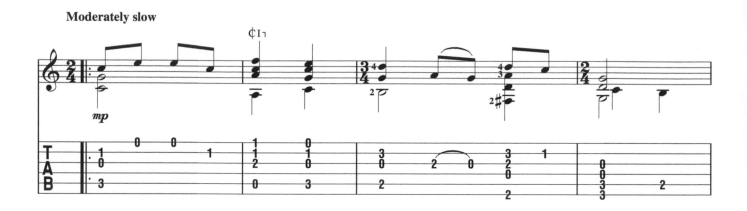

Fine

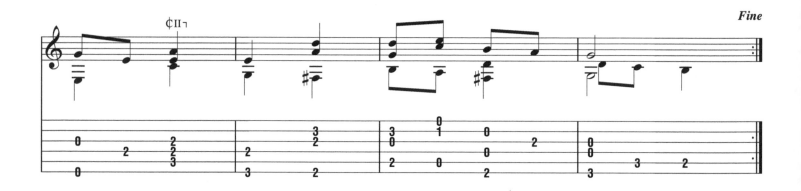

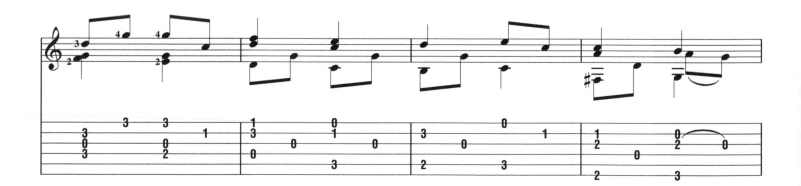

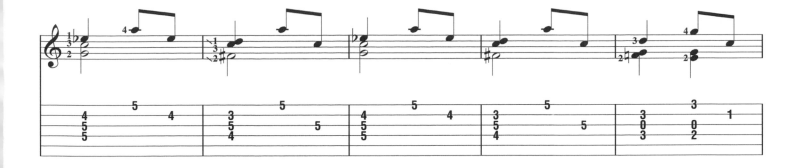

D.C. al Fine
(no repeat)

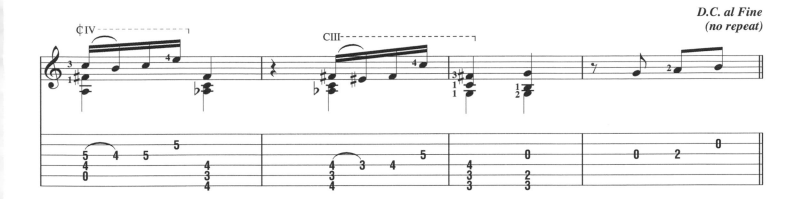

3

Arioso

Johann Sebastian Bach

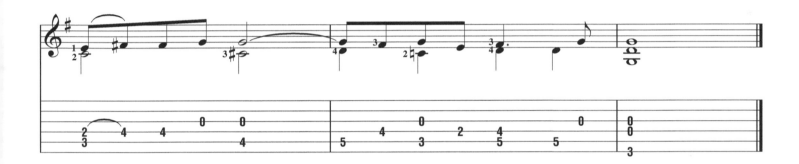

Ase's Death
from *Peer Gynt*

Edvard Grieg

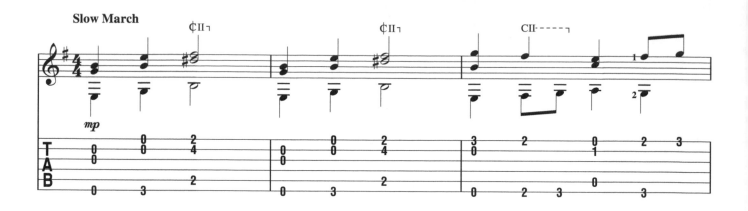

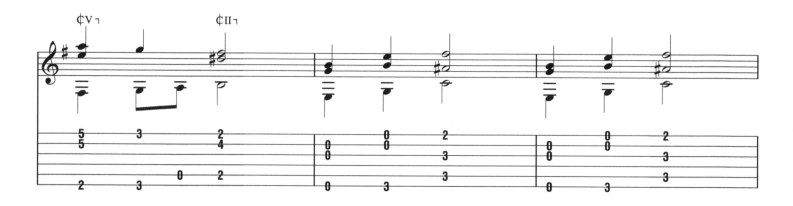

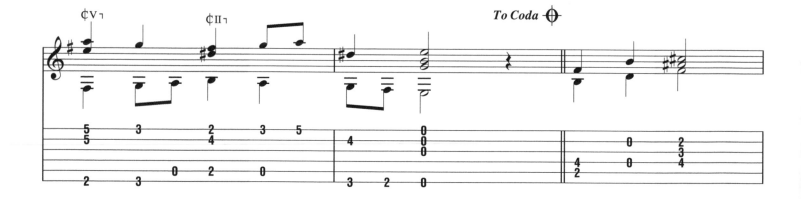

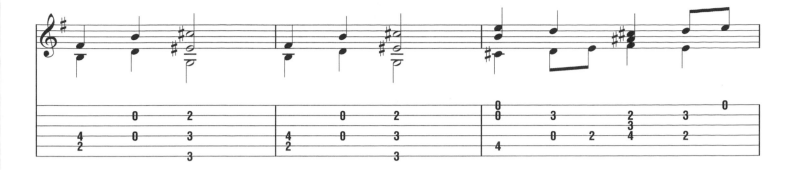

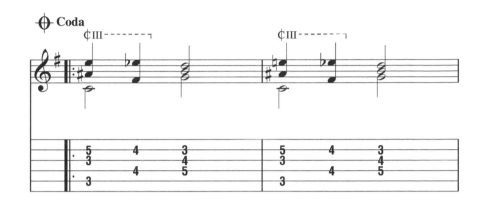

D.C. al Coda

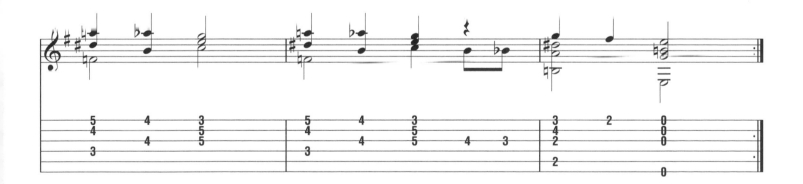

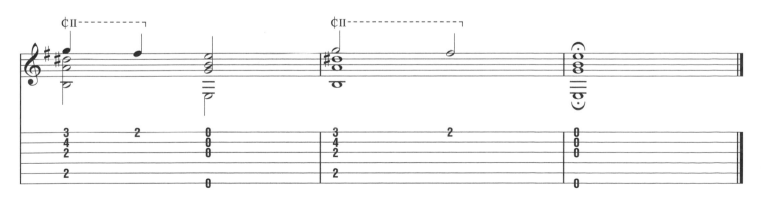

Ave Maria
based on "Prelude in C Major" by Johann Sebastian Bach

Charles Gounod

Moderately slow

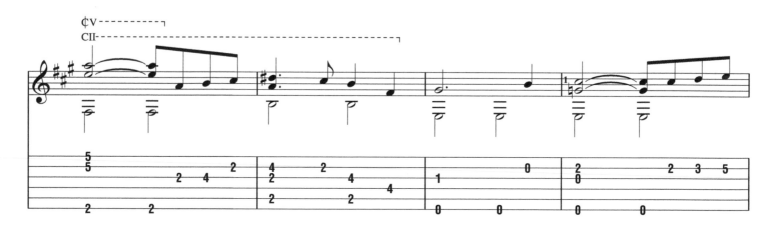

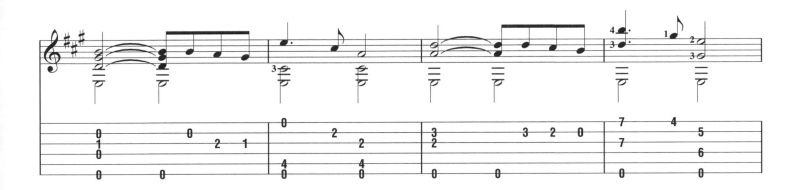

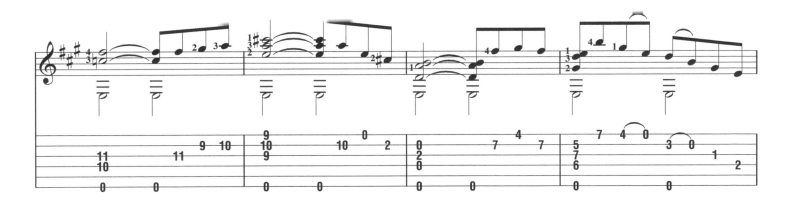

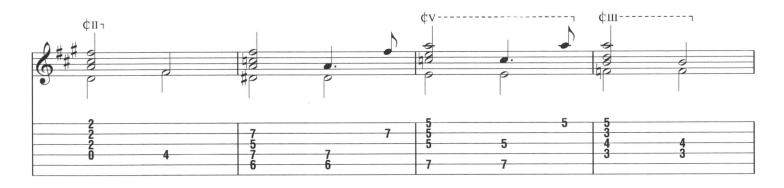

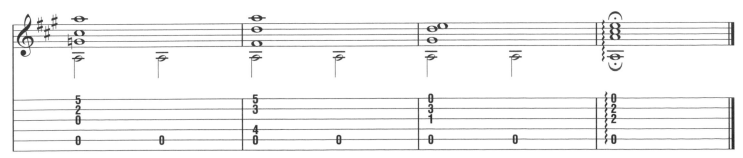

Air on the G String

Johann Sebastian Bach

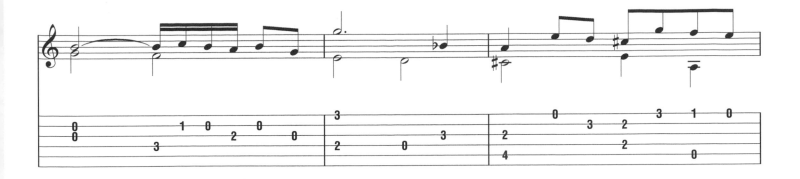

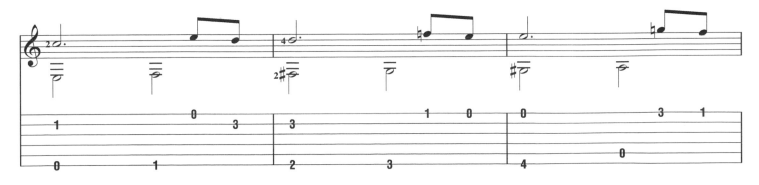

Ave Maria

Franz Schubert

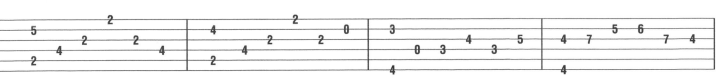

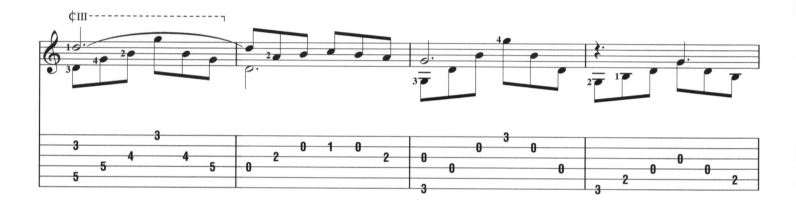

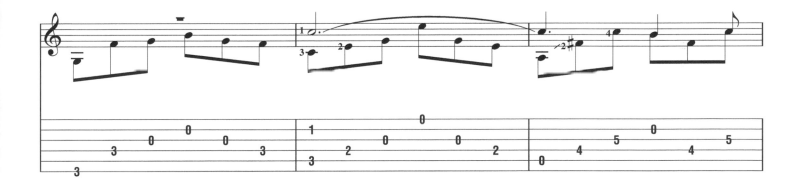

Ave Verum Corpus

Wolfgang Amadeus Mozart

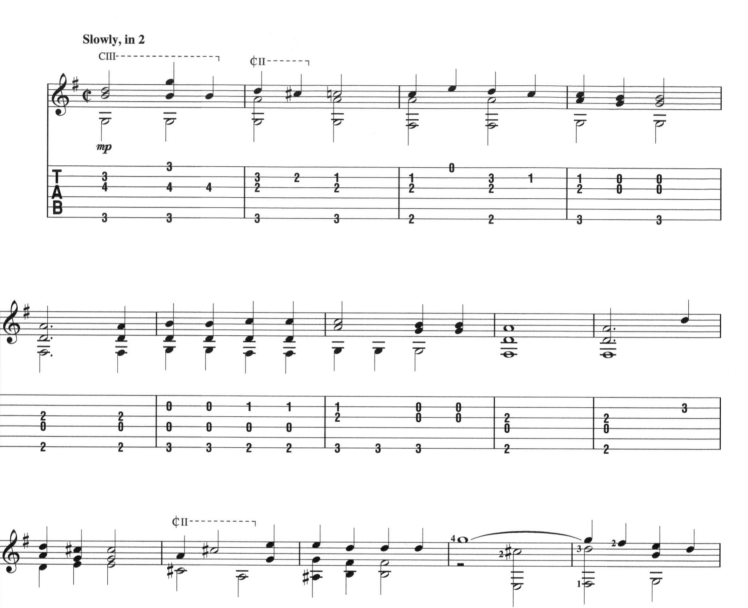

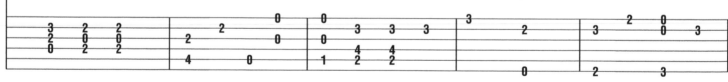

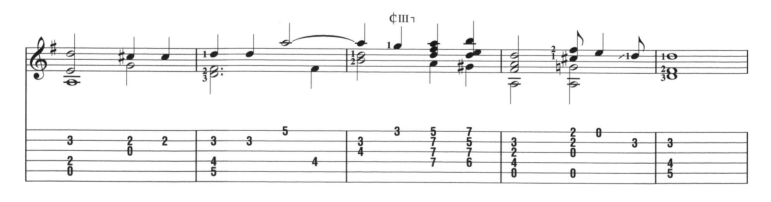

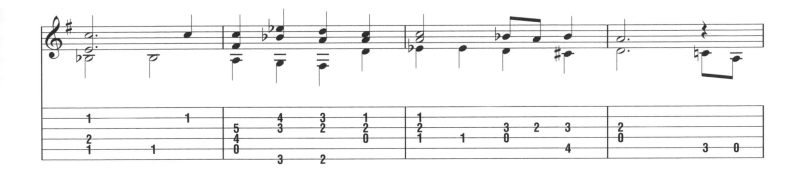

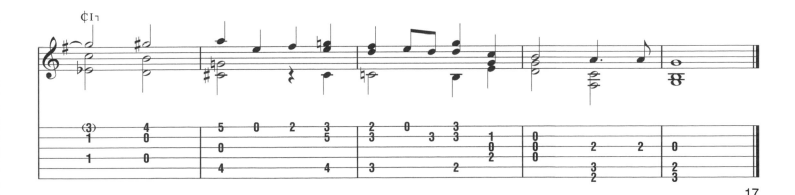

Be Thou with Me

Johann Sebastian Bach

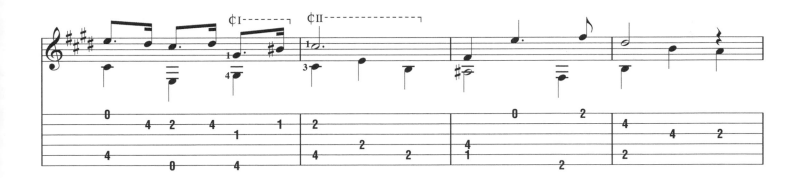

Canon in D

Johann Pachelbel

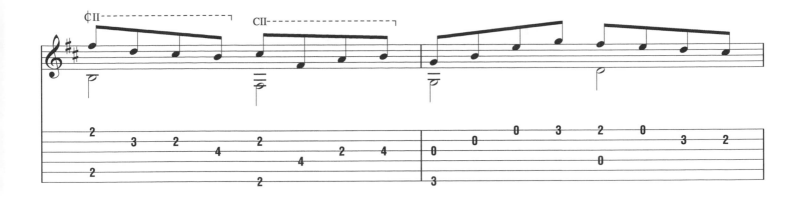

Cantique de Jean Racine

Gabriel Fauré

Moderately slow, in 2

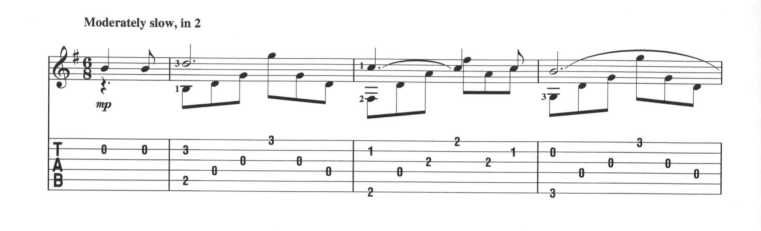

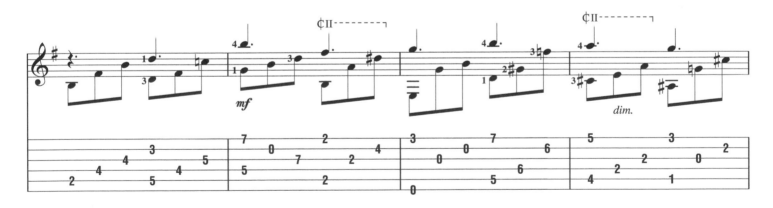

Caro mio ben

Giuseppe Giordani

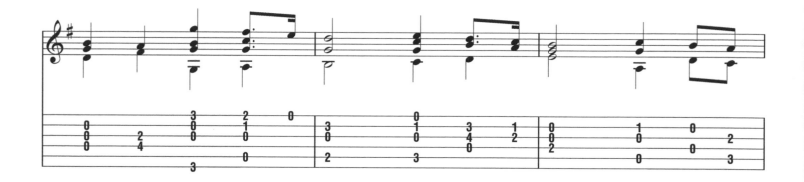

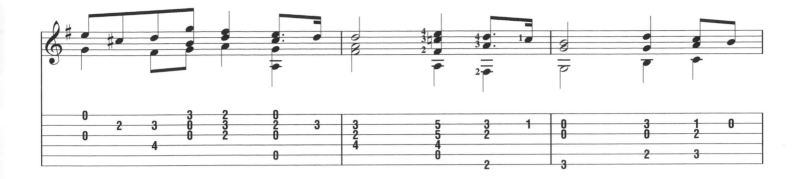

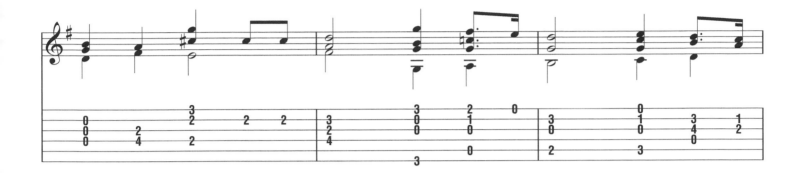

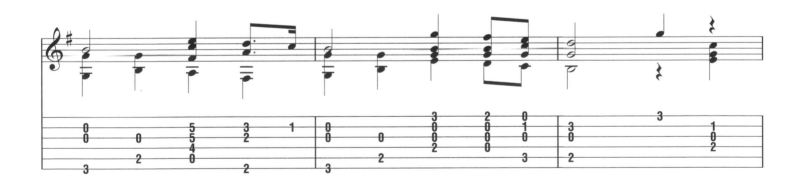

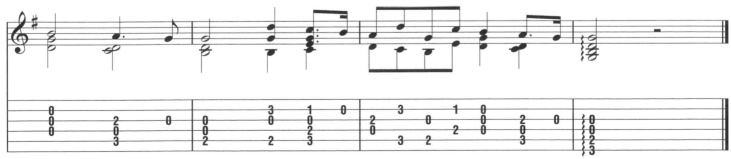

Clair de lune

Claude Debussy

Slowly, freely

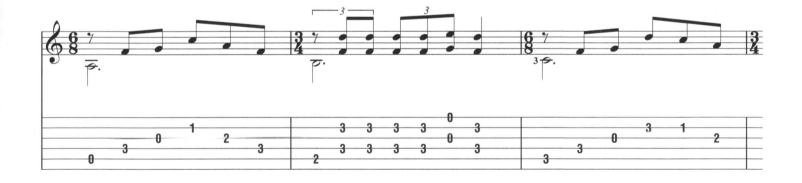

Chorale
from *St. Matthew Passion*

Johann Sebastian Bach

Moderately

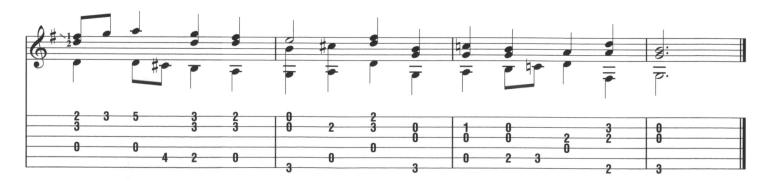

Dance of the Spirits

Christoph Willibald von Gluck

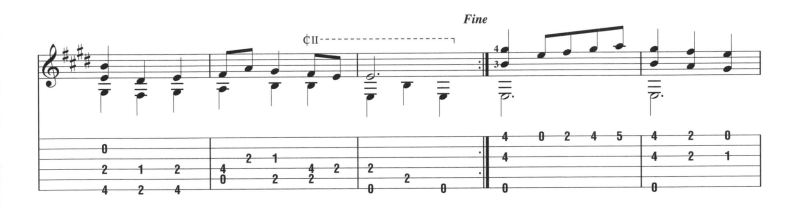

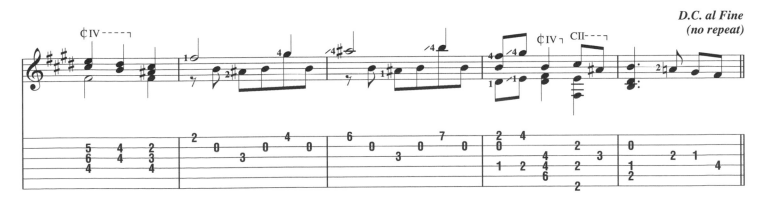

Evening Prayer
from *Hansel and Gretel*

Engelbert Humperdinck

Moderately, gently

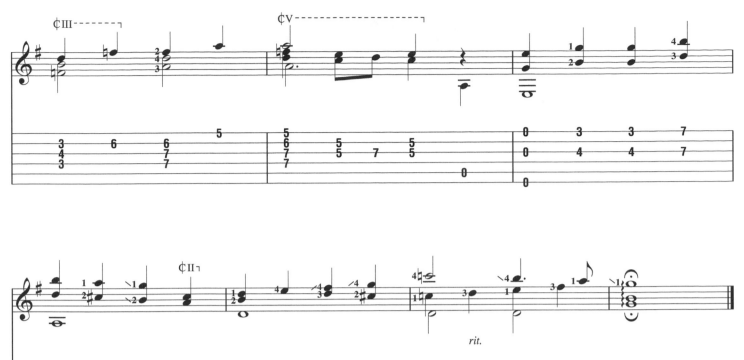

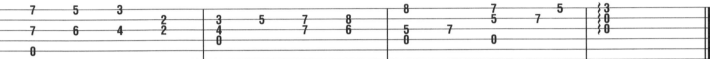

Gymnopédie No. 1

Erik Satie

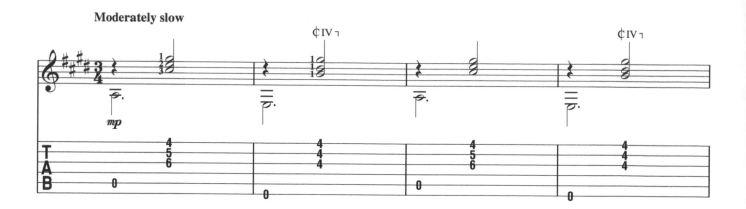

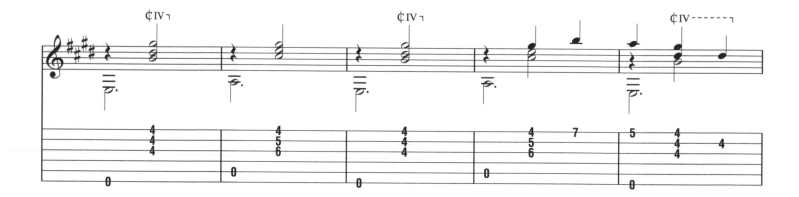

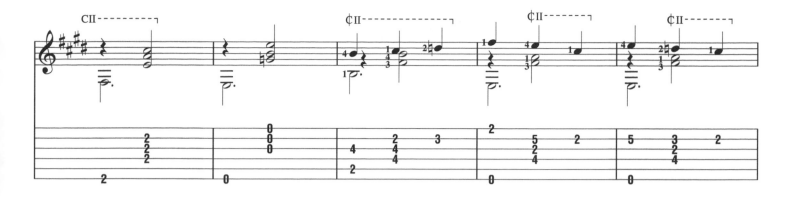

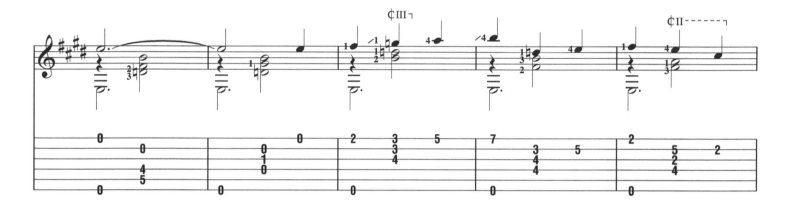

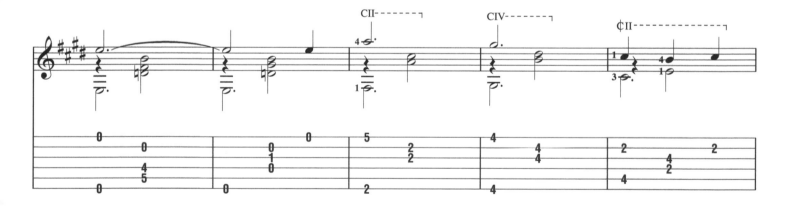

Für Elise

Ludwig van Beethoven

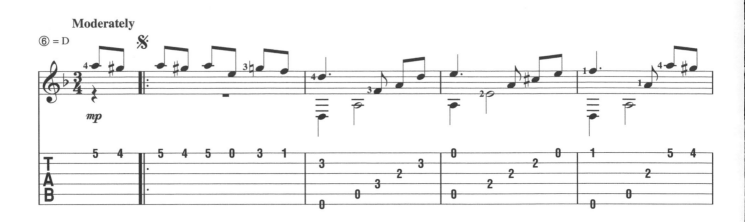

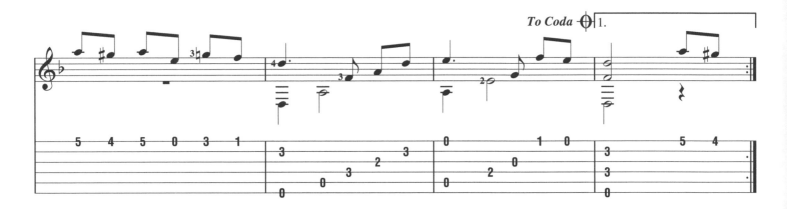

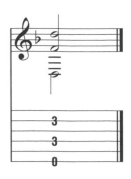

The Happy Farmer

Robert Schumann

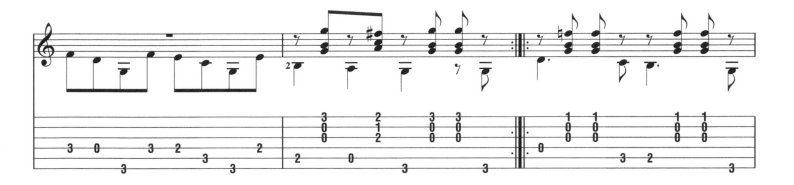

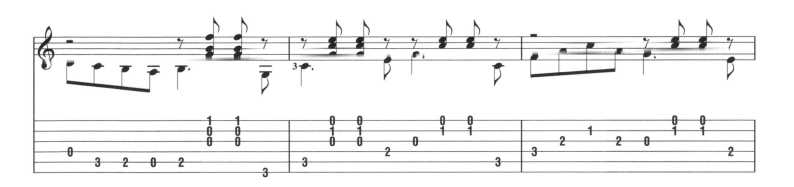

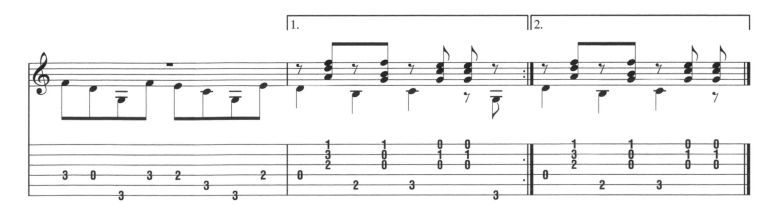

Intermezzo
from *Cavalleria rusticana*

Pietro Mascagni

Moderately slow

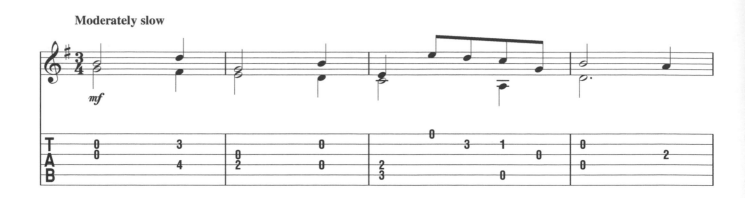

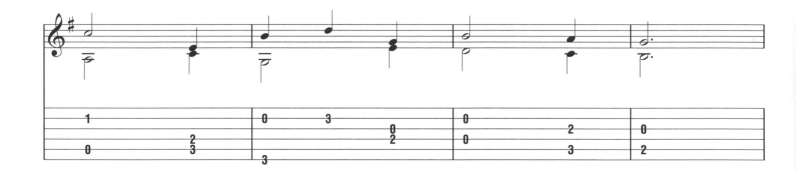

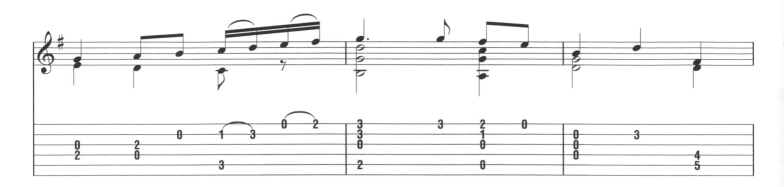

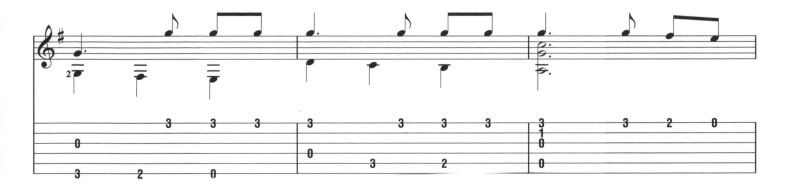

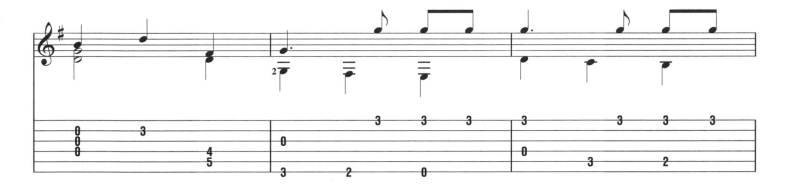

In the Hall of the Mountain King

from *Peer Gynt*

Edvard Grieg

Jerusalem

C. H. Parry

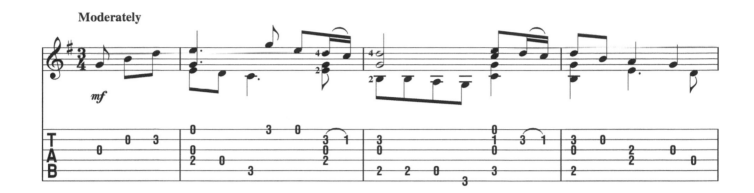

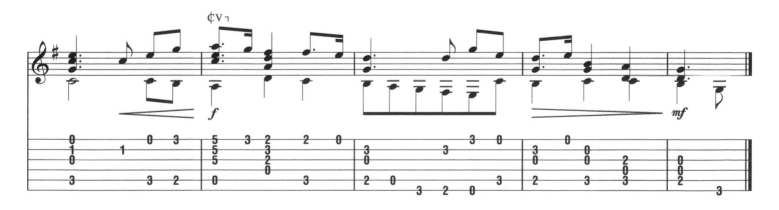

Jesu, Joy of Man's Desiring

Johann Sebastian Bach

Moderately slow

Fine

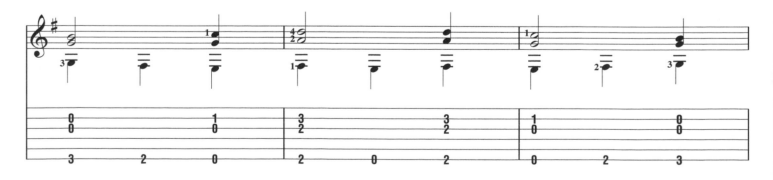

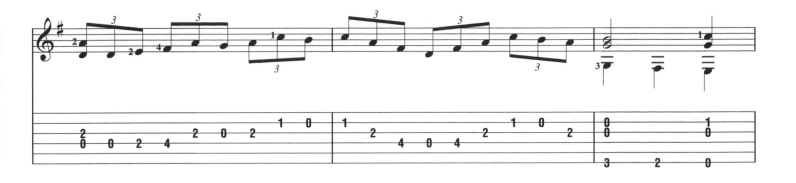

D.S. al Fine

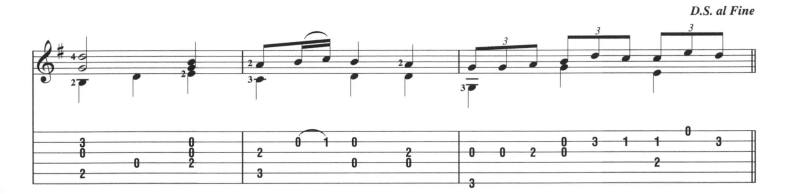

Keep, O My Spirit
from Christmas Oratorio

Johann Sebastian Bach

Moderately slow

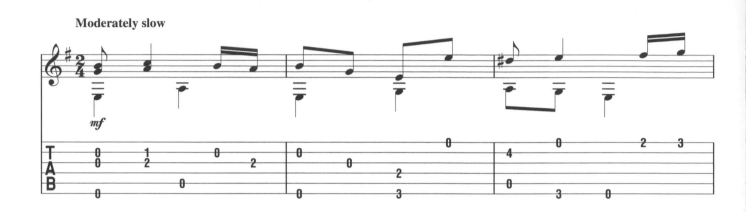

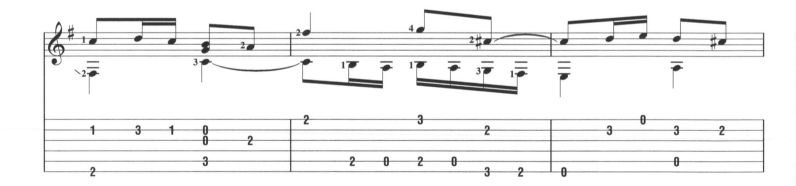

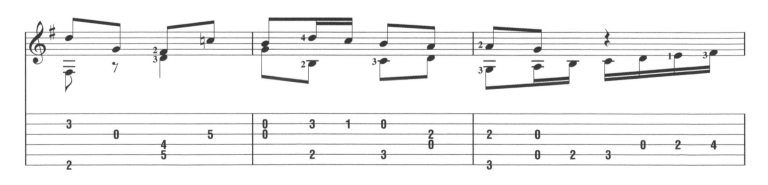

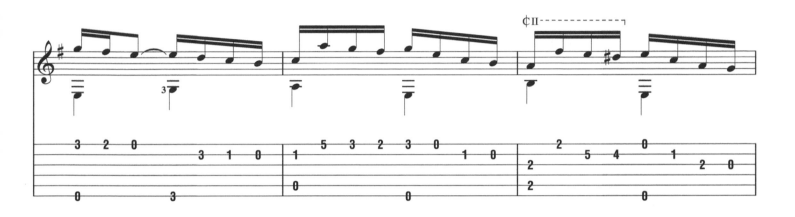

Klavierstuck

Wolfgang Amadeus Mozart

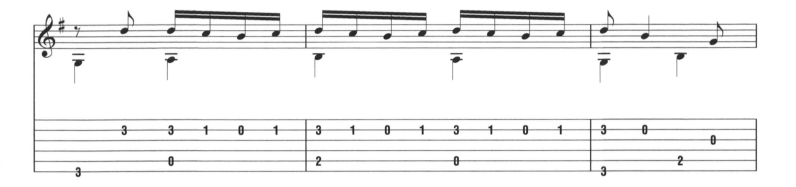

Minuet in G

Johann Sebastian Bach

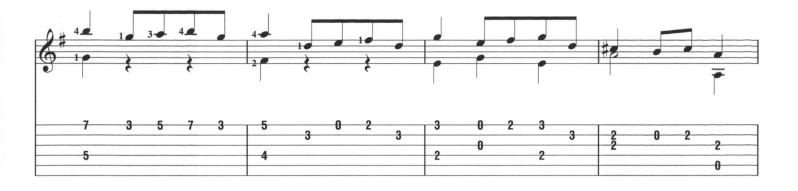

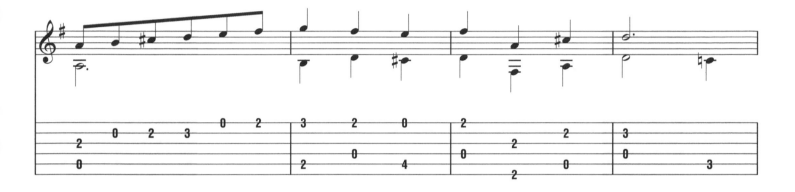

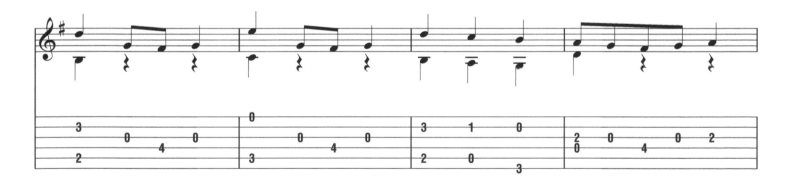

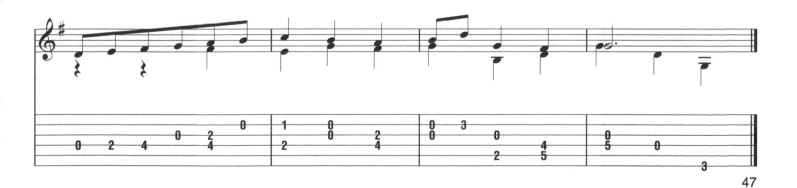

Lullaby

Johannes Brahms

Ode to Joy
from Symphony No. 9

Ludwig van Beethoven

Pie Jesu
from Requiem

Gabriel Fauré

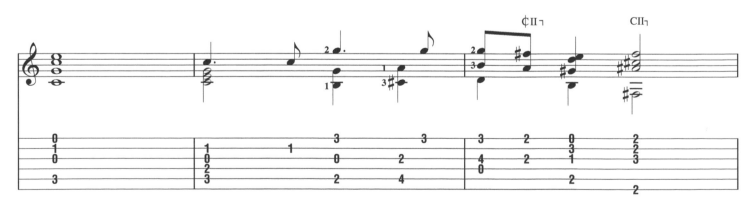

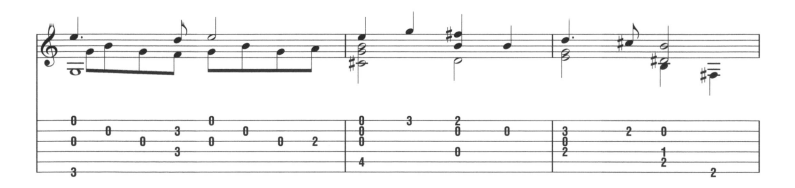

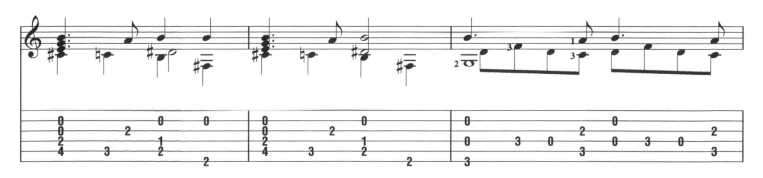

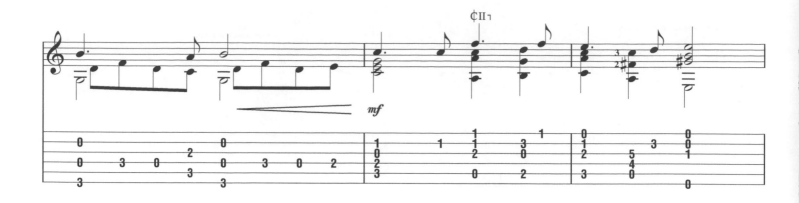

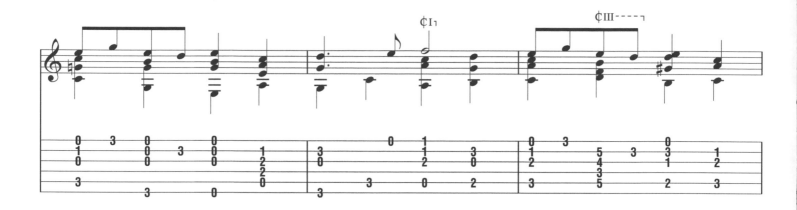

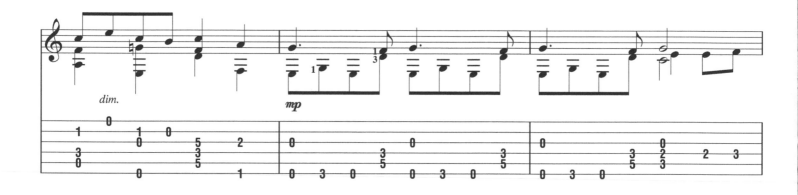

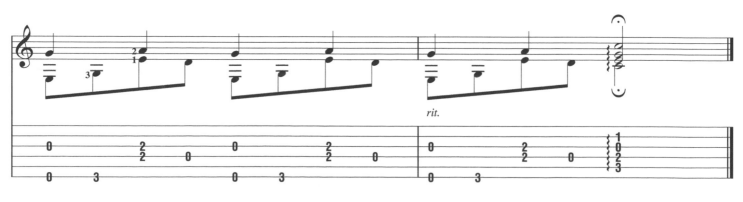

Rondeau

Jean-Joseph Mouret

Sleepers, Awake

Johann Sebastian Bach

Sonatina No. 5
Third Movement

Muzio Clementi

Moderately

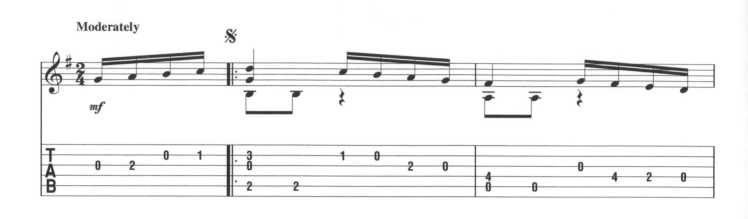

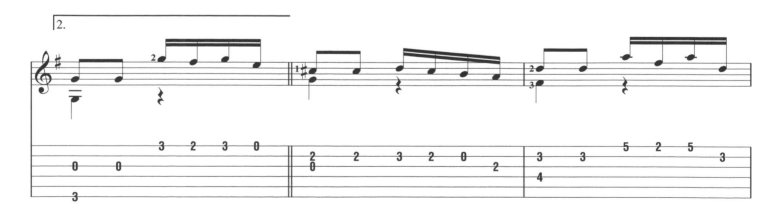

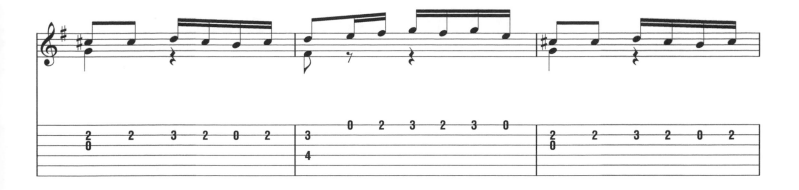

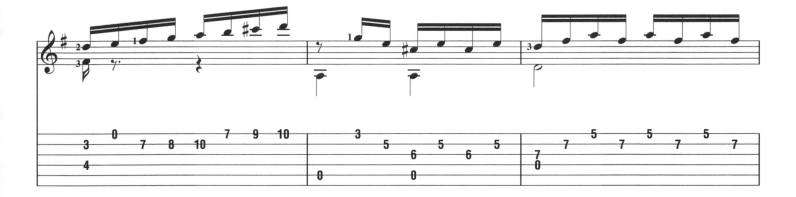

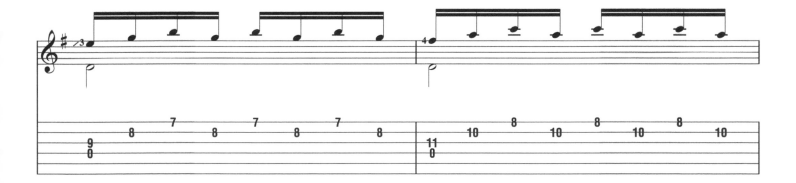

D.S. al Fine
(take 1st ending)

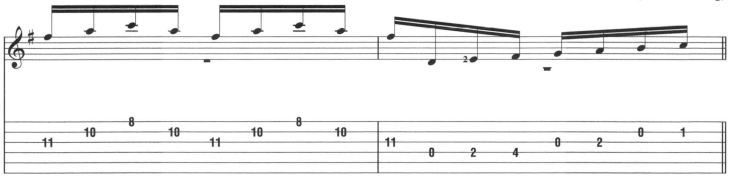

Sheep May Safely Graze

Johann Sebastian Bach

Moderately slow, in 2

The Surprise Symphony

Franz Joseph Haydn

Moderately slow

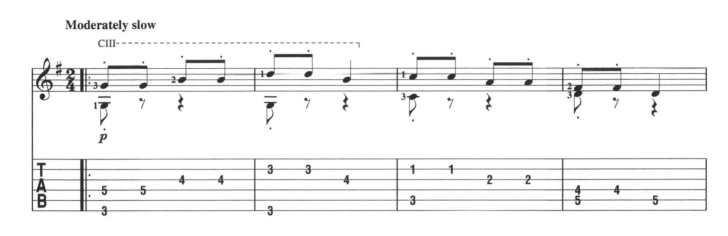

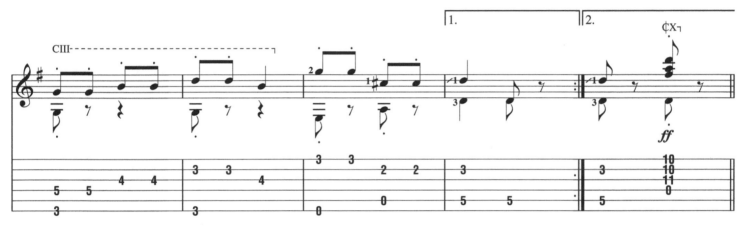

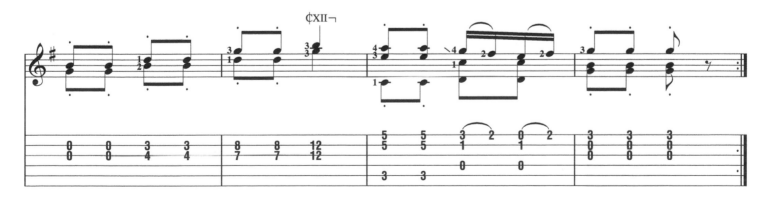

Symphony No. 5
(Second Movement)

Franz Schubert

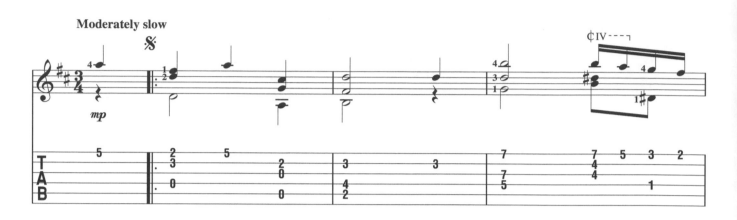

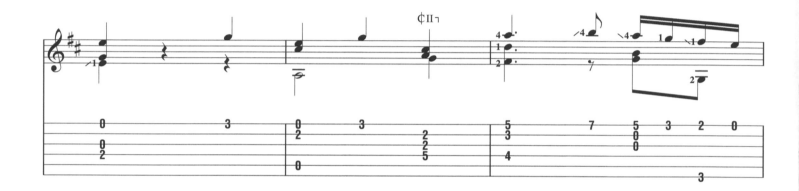

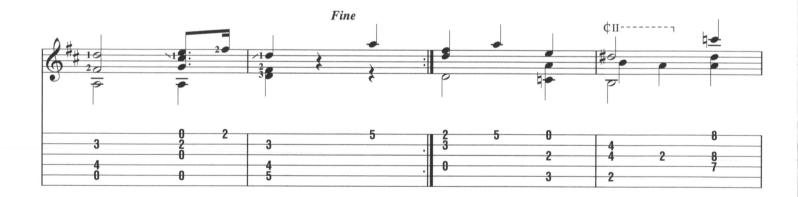

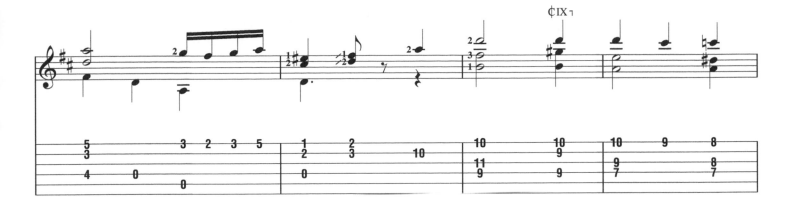

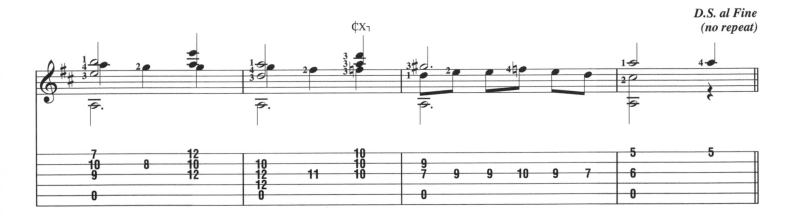

Symphony No. 9 in E Minor

"From the New World"

Second Movement

Antonin Dvořák

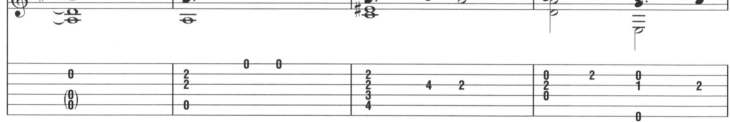

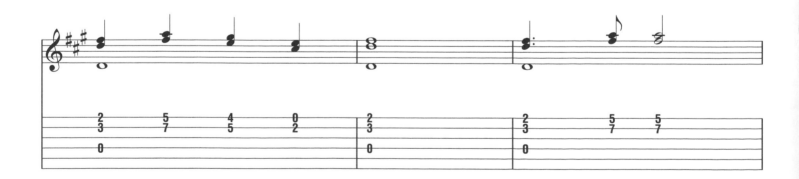

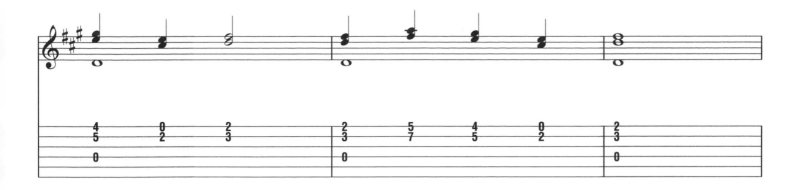

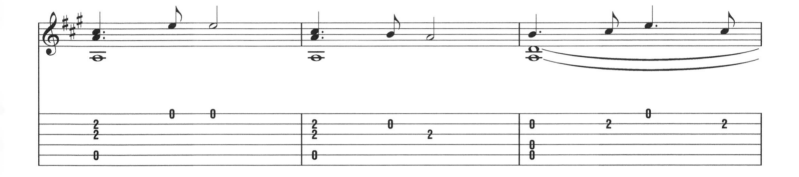

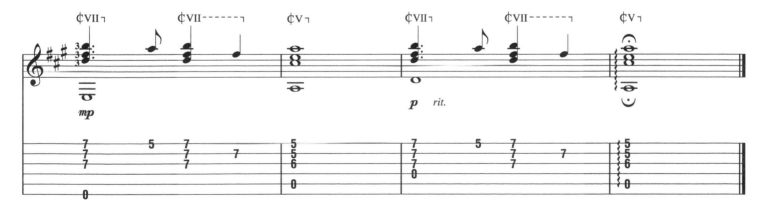

Symphony No. 3
Third Movement

Johannes Brahms

Moderately slow

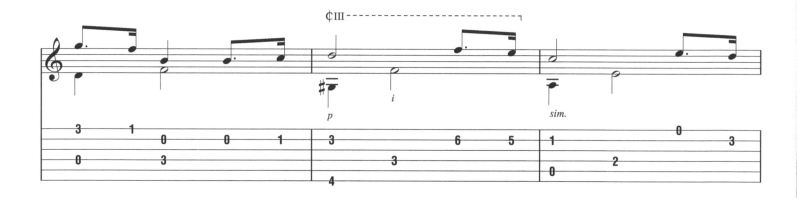

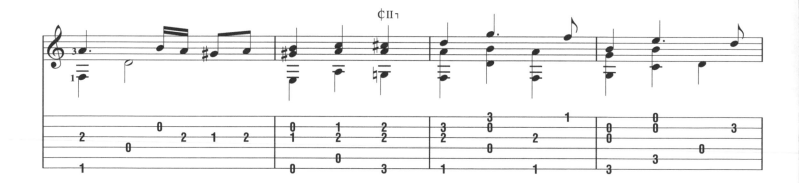

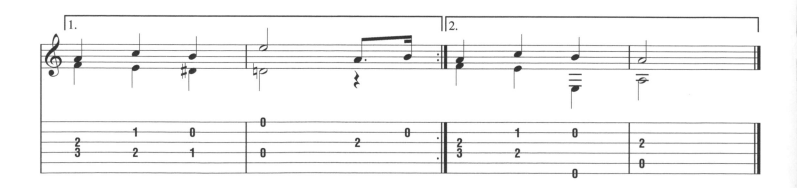